"Where was this ... ... ge? This is a must read f... ... tangible steps that will get them unstuck."

—Mike McRee, Vice President, LeaderShape Inc.

"T.J.'s strategy on how to deal with different levels of leadership engagement helped guide my organization to be more successful and effective. His philosophy of thirds is practical and easily relatable to any organization."

—Johnathan Jianu, ASI President,
Cal Poly Pomona

"Motivating the Middle is perfect for the busy student leader who needs a direct approach for motivating student groups. The concept of motivating the middle third of an organization, and the strategies found within T.J.'s book, are insightful. But even better, the concepts are usable, and the book contains just the right blend of readability and directness to assist student leaders in retention and productivity. This book will prove to be critical part of any student leader's motivation strategy."

—John A. Turner, Associate Dean of Student
Development, Lone Star College-Kingwood

Scott Ilbacher
November, 2011

"T.J. cuts to the essence by identifying the need for campus leaders to be energetic and also pragmatic. This addresses perhaps the most difficult aspect of leadership—understanding that some members will not share your passion and commitment and focusing your efforts on those who want to be engaged and involved."

—David Westol, Limberlost Consulting

"This should be required reading for any student leader in charge of an organization—a group in its infancy, or one that's been on campus for decades."

—Ray Harrell, Student Body President,
Marshall University

"Smart, simple, on target. An important concept for all student leaders to understand before they start banging their heads against the wall, trying to engage every member. The practical ideas will transform how they work, achieve results, and avoid burn out."

—Lori Hart, PhD

"I commiserated about member apathy with fellow hyper-involved student leaders every year. T.J. offers a brilliant and simple solution. This will save you unnecessary stress and frustration, and ultimately allow you to accomplish your goals."

—Sarah Shook, Student Body President,
University of Minnesota

"Insightful. Only an hour to read it, and it was like receiving a crash course in how to work with and motivate the different members of an organization. Loved this."

—Ashley Imdieke, Panhellenic President,
St. Cloud State University

MOTIVATING THE MIDDLE

Fighting Apathy
in College Student Organizations

T.J. SULLIVAN

Motivating the Middle: Fighting Apathy in College Student Organizations

Published by Wheatmark®

1760 E. River Road, Suite 145, Tucson, Arizona 85718 U.S.A.

www.wheatmark.com

ISBN: 978-1-60494-690-1 (paperback)

ISBN: 978-1-60494-691-8 (Kindle)

LCCN: 2011936263

To Rich Yoegel, a top-third guy.

A horse is dangerous at both ends and
uncomfortable in the middle.

Ian Fleming

CONTENTS

1

THIRDS

EVERY college student organization has thirds.

Top-third members do most of the work. They are the visible, busy leaders. If their hands are not actively doing something for the group, their minds are likely thinking about the next event, meeting, or project. They run for office. They step up when there is a need.

Top-third members are the student leaders. They make your organization a cornerstone of their campus identities. People recognize them, in large part, based on their involvement in your group.

John is a Delta Sig.

Carrie is in SGA.

Shauna is an RA over in Cravens Hall.

Darnell plays club rugby.

Top-third members always have an opinion about the direction of their organization or group, and they exert their influence and social capital to affect it. The success or failure of your organization reflects on them, personally. They will sit in someone's room, late into the night, discussing the politics of your organization, solving problems, or planning the next event.

Look at a top-third member's online profile, and you'll know immediately the level of his or her involvement and commitment to the organization. They wear the T-shirts, they care about new members, they work the table at the student involvement fair, they put a strong effort into fundraisers, and they can be competitive when the success of your group is on the line.

A top-third member gets very excited when the group does well and can get very frustrated or upset when it does badly. A top-third member cares deeply about the behavior and effort of other members, especially when it detracts from the group's success. Top-third members might place so much priority on the success of an event or project that their grades might suffer. A top-third member wishes everyone would take the organization more seriously and give 100 percent.

You are reading this book, and that probably means

you are a top-third member of some campus organization. It could be a sorority or the student newspaper, a sports team, a living community, the marching band, a small choir, or a big university committee. You want your fellow members to be motivated, to like each other, and to work well together. You want your organization to be the best.

You care about your group's campus image. You want more students on campus to know and appreciate your group for the good things it does. You might wish there were more resources—money or members, perhaps—so your group could do more.

You honestly love certain aspects of your organization, you see the potential it has, and you devote a large amount of time to its activities. You also see its shortcomings, and you earnestly strive to find fixes and constantly improve your group.

If your organization wins an award this year, it will be due, in part, to your efforts.

You go to leadership conferences, you read leadership blogs, and you understand how your personal efforts and choices impact the group.

When you graduate, you want your efforts to be remembered. Many of your best memories of college will be of times spent with your fellow members. You will always care about your group, and you hope it achieves great things when you're gone.

Operating in extreme contrast are your bottom-third members. Bottom-third members, for whatever reason, are the least likely to care or personally sacrifice for the organization. These are the members who might behave badly at an event, avoid paying their dues, publicly criticize the group, shirk their commitments, and create endless drama.

Bottom-third members make top-third members crazy. While you consistently go above and beyond, making enormous personal investments of time and energy to build your organization up, the bottom-third members miss no opportunity to rip it down and make it weaker. They don't show up to things. Or when they do, they are negative, or detract from the activity. They might only come around for the fun stuff—blowing off meetings, service events, or any other activity that might require effort. Sometimes, they sign up, but they bail.

For some organizations, bottom-third members are the ones who are technically members but never actually engage with the organization. You might never have even met these people. They are on the roster, you assume they get the emails, but they are like ghosts.

Bottom-third members don't seem to care much about the organization, or they might only care to the extent that it serves their needs. They come to the party, but they ditch the committee work. They frequently complain but never contribute toward solving any problems. They are the first to criticize your organization's leaders, perhaps actively interfering and hurting the organization's progress, but they never step up to lead.

Bottom-third members might have terrible attitudes. You wish you could roll back the clock and make it so they never joined. You dream of how nice everything could be if they'd quit and go away. Even so, you wish you could figure out how to make them productive members. You wish you could stop their negativity or harmful behavior and turn their attitudes around. You wish you could figure out how to motivate them, get them to show up and pitch in.

You spend a lot of your time worrying about bottom-third members—dealing with their drama, mitigating the problems they cause, and trying to understand why they feel and act the way they do. You take their negative influence and apathy personally. Tension exists between you and them. You don't feel like you are on the same team.

And so goes the dynamic of most student organizations.

Top-third members spend most of their time doing all the work, focused on their tasks, and wishing they could change the bottom third.

Bottom-third members spend most of their time focused on themselves, taking from the organization whatever small amount of value they find in it, and putting themselves constantly at odds with the top-third leaders.

Top-third members get exhausted and burnt out.

Bottom-third members give very little or nothing at all.

Top-third members commiserate with their advisors and get angry or depressed.

Bottom-third members make excuses and get drunk at the parties.

Top-third members try to solve issues.

Bottom-third members appear lazy and uncommitted.

Top-third members complain.

Bottom-third members complain.

And then, there is the forgotten third—the members in the middle.

2

THE
MIDDLE THIRD

CHRIS loves his fraternity. He shows up to almost all of the mandatory things, and he counts the brothers among his best friends. Brothers think of him favorably, but he's not really seen as a chapter leader. He held a committee chairmanship once but didn't pursue anything after that. He sometimes struggles with the financial and time commitments and frequently worries about all the things he needs to get done. His girlfriend complains about the amount of time he spends "doing fraternity."

Sarah has always enjoyed being an active member of Hillel. Last year, she went to everything, but this year, school has been a big challenge. Her accounting class is a nightmare, and on top of it all, her mom's health has been shaky. As much as she wants to attend meetings and social events, she finds herself craving sleep more.

Terrence was happy to accept an open student senate position because his advisor suggested it was a great opportunity. So far, however, he hasn't made much of a mark in that role. He goes to school on a predominantly white campus, and because he's a student leader of color, he gets asked to do a lot of things—from prospective student days to serving on college committees. His favorite night of the week is the one where he's got nowhere to be and can just play basketball with his friends. Those evenings seem few and far between.

Amy instantly became a rising star when she started at a two-year college. By her second semester, she was making such an impression that she seemed a natural to chair the campus sexual assault prevention committee. When she came back for her second year, she had taken a new job. She still attended most of the meetings, but she strongly rejected the notion that she might take over as chair. She's looking forward to transferring to a nearby four-year school when the current year ends.

Michelle got interested in the program board when she started her first year, and she's served on the films committee and the diversity week committee. But, she also works at a store in the nearby mall, and the money she makes there goes a long way toward helping with tuition bills and expenses. There's an opportunity to run for a chairman's position with the program board, but there's also an assistant manager's position potentially opening at the store. She doubts she can do both.

Puni writes for the student newspaper, covering the campus fine arts scene. Her work is great, and people like her in the newsroom. After each issue is put to bed, many of the writers, photographers, and editors enjoy socializing together. Puni avoids these gatherings, partly because she doesn't drink and partly because she feels more comfortable with her smaller group of close friends she's known since high school. When discussion of editor positions begin, Puni's name is barely considered because people don't feel like they know her as well as some of the other candidates.

There is a big space between top-third and bottom-third members, and it's in this forgotten space that the middle-third members live. Their perspective is different from that of both the top and bottom-third members.

If you've ever caught yourself thinking that a very small percentage of your members do all of the work, that indicates that you are failing to properly activate and motivate your middle third.

Middle-third members care about your organization or team. Unlike bottom-third members, they have a positive attitude and they want contribute. They simply want to do it in a way that fits with their lives and other demands. Unlike top-third members, involvement in your organization is not the defining element of their personal identities. Your organization is a priority for them, but not always their top one. They might have a job, a relationship, a group of close friends outside your organization, a challenging academic situation, or a stronger commitment to another campus or community organization.

Because they are not the first to step up, take control, or activate a solution, we don't typically think of middle-third members as leaders of our organizations. They don't seek praise, responsibility, or attention. They don't offer a ton of opinions, and they don't criticize. They fly under the radar. A middle-third member is happy to contribute to the success of the organization, but is much more likely to be a supporting player than the MVP.

A middle-third member likes certain aspects of your organization more than others. He might enjoy the intramurals but dislike the meetings. She might love the community service and dislike the large group events. He might like the actual work of your organization but avoid the social elements that take place outside of regular business. When your group has an event, your top-third members wouldn't miss it. It's a given that they will be there. Middle-third members make a decision to be there and might choose to skip tomorrow's event because they made it to today's.

They have many different things going on, and those things don't always mesh seamlessly. Frequently, they have to choose between priorities, which means your organization doesn't always win out. Middle members are jugglers. They have multiple priorities that compete for their time, attention, and energy. When they come to your leadership event, they've had to move other things around to do it. They put off other people or other opportunities in their life outside of your group to make it happen.

Some jugglers are better than others.

One middle member is doing a great job of handling the multiple demands in her life. Another is struggling as soon as one priority becomes more demanding or when something unexpected—a tough class, trouble in a relationship, a nasty case of the flu—comes along. But, they are all keenly aware that the balance is delicate and easily thrown off. As they juggle, they keep a wary eye on anything that might throw things off.

The middle member will do what he needs to do, or the parts he finds enjoyable and rewarding, but he won't be signing up for leadership positions that might demand a lot more of him. If your meeting is supposed to last for an hour, and instead goes for two, the middle-third member gets annoyed. You've just thrown off his balance. When a volunteer is needed, a middle-third member's hand usually doesn't go up, particularly if the parameters of the role are vague. It's OK, because a top-third member is going to volunteer anyway. Or, a middle-third member might approach a leader later, casually, and ask if any help is needed. A middle-third member doesn't throw out ideas at meetings because she might get saddled with more to do.

At the same time, a middle-third member doesn't cause problems because he cares about your organization and wants to be supportive. Middle-third members get excited about the successes, and they worry about the failures and shortcomings. They look to the top-third members to set things right, then they follow that lead.

Sometimes a middle-third member feels guilty. He sees top-third members, the leaders of your group, working hard, and he wishes he could do more. But, the juggling demands he stands a step back. He will likely pitch in when really needed or when a bottom-third member is on the attack, but most days he goes with the flow.

When you suggest a middle-third member take a larger role, she might turn you down. A middle-third member likely does not feel capable of putting in the same energy, enthusiasm, or time that a top-third member does. A middle-third member might simply be shy or less than fully confident in his abilities. A supporting role is a safer place. A middle-third member might be the type of person to avoid conflict and drama. Therefore, when top-third and bottom-third members are going at it, the middle-third member appreciates the safety of remaining uninvolved.

When a middle-third member is "struggling with the juggling," stress happens. If one life priority gets out of whack, other things are going to suffer and be neglected. Unlike the bottom third, a middle-third member hates drama. In fact, drama that results in more stress and wasted time can drive away middle-third members. A middle-third member likes your organization when it's working and when it's pleasant. He is more attuned to the emotional feel of your organization than either the top or bottom third. But if involvement in your organization starts feeling negative, then the middle-third member might show up less, help out less, resign that leadership position, or spend more time with people he enjoys more. While the top and bottom thirds scream at each other, the middle-third member is keeping an eye on the door.

Top-third members of your organization get the glory, the responsibility, and the majority of the stress. Everyone has their cell phone numbers. Bottom-third members might have the most fun, get the most negative attention, and the least responsibility. The least is expected of them. The middle-third member exists in the safe space in the middle. These members are allowed to handle multiple priorities without anyone, including your organization, dominating. They get to be involved without the high pressure of responsibility. They get the benefits without drawing a huge amount of attention to themselves.

Middle-third members demand very little, and the performance expectation is modest. They maintain relationships, help out when needed, and maintain a low-maintenance attitude. They get the enjoyment of the organization without accepting as much of the stress. They are generally liked but rarely put upon.

As you think about the thirds, you might realize that you're a top third member in one organization, a middle-third member in another, and a bottom-third member in another. This is especially common at smaller schools where students are part of a lot of different organizations.

If you are a student leader at an urban campus or a campus where many people have jobs, you might be thinking, "Everybody is a middle-third member in my organization! Everyone is juggling!" That might be true, and the distinctions between the thirds might be much more subtle. But, if you stop and really analyze it, you'll note that there are those who invest at different levels of intensity.

If your organization is struggling, you might think, "Everyone is in the bottom third!" But, that's probably not true. If you stop and analyze, you'll see those who are working to turn things around, those who are standing in the neutral zone waiting to follow, and those who are making the problems worse.

Regardless of where a member of your organization falls in this concept of thirds, that person is there for a reason. There are positives and negatives for people in each category. Where you fall in a particular organization is almost never accidental.

So here you are, a top-third member, having been elected to office or otherwise facing the challenges of leading your organization, and you want to know how to motivate everyone, make change, and move your organization forward. If you could make everyone into top-third members, this would be easy. Of course, that's impossible. You're going to have folks in all three places. You can spend your time wishing everyone would join you in the top third, or you can start strategically dealing with people where they are.

3

MOTIVATE
THE MIDDLE

THE single biggest mistake that student organization leaders (top-third members) make when it comes to motivation and fighting apathy is thinking that all of their members will respond to the same things that motivate them.

Top-third student leaders like awards, so they try giving awards. They enjoy praise, so they create elaborate recognition programs. Top-third student leaders feel a sense of duty and obligation to their organization and are amazed that others don't feel as strongly. We plead, lecture, and guilt our members.

When these motivational techniques fail, we begin to call our members apathetic. Soon, top-third student leaders make events and meetings mandatory.

They begin looking down on members who don't have the same level of commitment, and, soon, fines are levied, and less-involved members are threatened with expulsion.

Top-third student leaders take involvement in your group very personally. We just don't understand why other people don't *want it* as badly as we do. *What are we doing wrong?*

Here's what's wrong. You forget that the other two-thirds see your organization in a different framework. They aren't motivated by the same things that motivate you. Your best friends in the organization are likely also top-third members, and they are motivated by the same things as you. With your fellow top-third members you continue the awards, the recognitions, and the increases of responsibility. You praise them, publicly applaud their good work, and give them opportunities like attending conferences on behalf of the organization. You give them lots of rewards for all they do, and they continue to give 100 percent to the organization. But, for the most part, this won't work with middle-third members.

Middle-third members care about the organization, but they worry. They worry about their leadership abilities, they worry about not being able to handle the other priorities in their lives, or they simply prefer to play a supporting role. They can be motivated, however. You have to motivate them in ways that match their needs and their roles in the group's hierarchy. Here are thirteen motivational examples.

1. Ask their opinion, but don't ask them to do anything else. Start off the conversation with, "I want to pick your brain, if you have some time. Don't worry. I'm not going to ask you to take on any responsibilities. I just value your opinion."

2. Ask, "What one thing do you think we could be doing that we aren't that would make this group stronger?" Then, listen to the idea. In some cases, the middle-third member might express interest in helping out, but don't expect her to. The main thing is that you are soliciting her opinion and taking it seriously. Middle-third members are not used to being asked for their ideas.

3. Nothing stresses out a middle-third member facing midterms like the prospect of a long, drawn-out meeting. Start and end your meetings on time. Make it a near-religious leadership commitment.

By beginning and ending on time, you earn trust of middle-third members, and you support their need to juggle priorities.

4. Invite the significant others. If your middle-third members are getting pushback from their partners about the time they spend with your organization, maybe you need to include them in more of your activities, particularly the social ones. Reach out and personally invite them to be a part of events. Encourage middle-third members to bring their significant others to events.

5. Middle members really hate mandatory events, even if they usually come to them. Giving them more choices and the ability to skip the things they don't enjoy will increase their enjoyment and commitment.

6. Minimize the conflict in your group to the greatest extent possible. The constant ego battles between top- and bottom-third members wear out the middle-third members, who would frankly rather get back to the business of the organization. All the attention you give to the badly behaving bottom-

third members is time and focus you could be giving your middle third.

7. Let a middle-third member lead on the thing he likes most. Many middle members will surprise you and will step up to lead if an opportunity matches something they enjoy. The problem is, the thing they enjoy might not be something you're doing right now or have ever done. Find out what the middle-third members get excited about, and then see if your organization can try it.

8. Thank them for participating. The top-third members are always the ones hogging the praise and spotlight. Start making a habit of thanking your middle members for their attendance and participation. "Kevin, I really appreciate that you're always contributing so much to our intramural program. Just wanted you to know."

9. Offer to assist with other stressful areas. If your middle member is struggling with molecular biology, is there someone you can identify who can lend a hand? Middle-third members can be so busy juggling that they feel embarrassed to ask for

help. Less stress in one area can mean more energy available to devote to your organization.

10. Give them a meaningful supporting role. "The treasurer could really use some assistance. Would you be willing to step in for a few days and help him get caught up?" A top-third member might not take on any role without a title and some power, but a middle-third member might feel great doing a very low-key task that helps the organization.

11. Ask for help on one specific, limited-time task. Instead of expecting a middle-third member to take up a yearlong executive position, ask her to help with one specific task. "We have the alumni picnic coming up on the fifteenth, and I need someone I trust to make sure we get correct addresses, phone numbers, and emails for those who come. Can you help me with that?"

12. Take some personal time with them. The student senator representing the graduate school of business comes to most of the meetings, but you know nothing about her. Invite her to coffee. Show an interest. Answer questions she might have about

the organization, and share with her how you got involved. Let her know how she can share ideas directly with you instead of speaking up in front of the large group meeting.

13. Slow down on the decisions. If decisions are made quickly at meetings, your middle-members aren't contributing to them. Middle members don't like wrangling with top-third members in the heat of a meeting. Between the origination of an idea and a final decision, you should reach out to middle-third members for their suggestions and concerns. You can hardly expect middle-third members to support ideas in your organization if top-third members are dominating the entire process and excluding the thoughtful input from the middle third.

4

MIDDLE-MEMBER STRATEGY

IF you want to solve chronic problems or initiate change in your college student organization or campus community, you can use a Middle-Member Strategy. This can mean one of two things.

You can approach those who are middle members and strategize based on their ideas, wants, and needs. You assume that the top third is generally with you and the bottom third is generally against you, and you work to romance the middle. You do what it takes to get their buy-in, and, therefore, move the majority in your favor. Like a presidential candidate playing to independent voters, you have to play to the middle if you want change to happen.

The Middle-Member Strategy could also mean

identifying a particular chronic issue in your organization and then targeting the habits, behaviors, or opinions of those who fall in the middle on that particular problem. For example, you could improve attendance by appealing to those who attend most—but not all—of the time. You could increase the appeal of your student center by marketing to those who spend only a modest amount of time there. Following are some more examples of scenarios in which the Middle-Member Strategy might be useful.

Your sorority chapter would like to boost its cumulative grade point average. You could certainly take the approach of demanding that all sisters sit for study tables three nights a week with fines and threats for anyone who does not comply. But a wiser choice would be to make a list of your sisters in descending order with those with the best grades at the top of the page and those with the worst at the bottom. Draw lines dividing the list into thirds. Conventional wisdom says you should focus on the bottom third. Those with the worst grades need the most help, right?

No. If you want to create cultural change in your chapter and build value around higher grades, you should focus on the middle third. A bottom-third sister with a 1.2 GPA is unlikely to pull a 3.0 next semester. However, that middle-third sister with a 2.7 might achieve that 3.0 if given encouragement, incentive, and assistance.

Your student government is considering an increase in student activity fees, and you expect it to be controversial. People generally don't naturally get excited about fee or tuition increases. There are probably a third of representatives on your student government who will understand the argument for the increase and support the effort. You can think of these representatives and their organizations as your top third. They are probably going to vote your way if you give them a sound argument and involve them in the development of the proposal.

There will be a certain portion of representatives and organizations that will vote against the increase under any circumstances. It doesn't matter how rational the argument or how earnestly you work for their support. This is your bottom third, and some will be quite vocal in their opposition and may work hard to kill the idea.

The battle will be won or lost with the middle members—those representatives and organizations who see both sides. They will listen, they will form opinions, and they will watch the politics. Your ability to market the importance of an affirmative vote will steer them for or against the measure. To win them, you may need to negotiate or change an implementation schedule or allocate money to some new places at their asking.

If you expect them to go along reasonably like the top-third reps, your proposal will go down. You will need to take the conversation to them, ask for their ideas, allay their worries, and make the scales tip in your favor.

Your programming board has had one concert blunder after another. Your group keeps hiring bands that your officers love, but ticket sales just don't happen. You've tried different kinds of music, and you've tried different nights of the week. Nothing is working.

Your concerts committee is made up of top-third types—people who love music and who spend a lot of time learning what's hottest. They listen to things the rest of us haven't even heard of yet. They and their friends love the recent choices and start griping that the students on your campus have no musical taste.

To begin solving the problem, you interview and survey students who have been to concerts in the past but not lately. Maybe you seek out the students who come to other programming board events but not the concerts. These are students who probably like music and who might go to a concert but who haven't been buying tickets.

You discover that most of them prefer country music to the edgy rock bands your programming board has been hiring. You also find that they prefer outdoor concerts to ones held in your auditorium. Data from the surveys also indicate that your middle-member crowd would prefer something less edgy if it meant ticket prices could be lower.

If you ask people unlikely to attend a concert, you'll get nothing useful. If you continue to allow the concerts committee to make choices that only fit their narrow and nonpopulist choices, you will continue to lose money. Talk to the students in the middle who don't care deeply about campus concerts.

Every year, your campus has a student leadership conference on a Saturday in January right after everyone gets back from winter break. You are in charge of this year's conference.

The conference has been modestly successful, but attendance declines a bit every year. The fraternities and sororities always support the event, and, in fact, tend to dominate it a bit. Your advisor says that it would be great if student leaders from other campus organizations were better represented.

At your first committee meeting, you ask for ideas. Those on the committee (representing the top third) suggest things like better T-shirts, a more expensive lunch, or certain keynote speakers that they like.

You decide to set up casual meetings with leaders of student organizations who have stopped coming to the event. Some of them have bad attitudes about the event and have nothing but negative things to say about it (bottom third). You let them rant about how much the event sucks and how they would never come.

But, you listen to others who say they'd like to come but that participating is difficult (middle members). Some say that devoting a full Saturday to a leadership conference conflicts with their jobs. Others say that they will probably attend but don't find many sessions that apply to their organizations. Some say they just don't feel valued because the fraternities and sororities dominate.

You come to the conclusion that what you really need is two student leadership conferences. One on a Saturday that appeals to the larger organizations on campus and another on a weeknight that is shorter, invitation only so you can control the balance of organization types that are there, and more inclusive of organizations that don't often get attention.

You can apply the Middle-Member Strategy to almost any problem, campus organization, or leadership challenge.

Struggling with declining attendance at meetings? Instead of asking top-third members (who always come) or threatening bottom-third members (who hate coming), start finding out what changes you could make to make meetings more excited for the middle member who attends three meetings out of four. Should we change the time? Do we need to introduce more substantive topics?

Need to raise more money for your organization? Instead of doing the fundraiser that appeals to the top third (who will likely participate in whatever you end up doing), or begging the bottom third to participate (they aren't very motivated to raise anything for you), ask the middle third. How much time would they invest in a fundraiser? Would they be willing to sell tickets? What have they seen work that would take only a reasonable amount of time and effort.

Needing to change the campus mascot? Want to

increase attendance at Lacrosse games? Seeking ideas on a redesign of your campus center? Attempting to reshape your peer education organization?

Start with the middle.

5

ABOUT THE
BOTTOM THIRD

ALL of this talk about motivating the middle third inevitably leads to the question, *What about the bottom third? Do we just ignore them and let them get away with contributing less to the organization?*

The answer is yes . . . Pretty much, yes.

It comes down to a matter of purpose. Your mission as the leader of your student organization is to advance the mission of your group—to serve your members, to move things forward, and to leave the organization stronger than you found it. You don't accomplish this by spending all of your time servicing a group of people who demonstrate weak commitment, who engage in harmful behavior, or who disrespect the organization and its leadership.

Every organization has bottom-third members. When we think of a bottom-third member, we tend to think of the nasty person with a personality disorder who makes us (top-third members) crazy. We think of the person who elicits the most negative emotional response from us as the "model" bottom-third member.

Realistically, those who are now bottom-third members might not have always been. Many members we would fairly consider "bottom third" have checked out for understandable reasons. Some have simply moved on, or have become alienated. Some others might act terribly toward the group because of hurt feelings or because they perceive that promises have been broken. They joined when the group was one way, and now the group has changed. Top-third members see these changes as a good for the organization, but bottom-third members do not.

Bottom-third members might have something going on in their lives that don't leave room for involvement in our organization. A parent with cancer, an unplanned pregnancy, or a traumatic end to a relationship might cause a member to withdraw. Who knows?

A former officer might have been there, done that, and moved on. A newer member might have just discovered a campus involvement that speaks more to his passions. A young gay man might avoid his fraternity because he feels unwelcome in the chapter's social activities. A young woman recovering from a life-changing sexual assault might care more about those issues than formal sorority recruitment.

There are countless reasons why someone might fall into the bottom third. It might be intentional, or it might be simply necessary in their minds. Most of the time, it has nothing to do with you.

Sometimes, it has everything to do with you. A member who ran against you for president can't stand you, and now that you've won, they have nothing but venom. It happens. When a person no longer enjoys being a member and for whatever reason chooses to stop making an effort, it's a waste of everyone's time to focus excessive energy on her. If they are asking for help, or if they need a little flexibility from you, that's a different matter. But when they have checked out, or when they are actively engaged in hurting the organization, you should direct your energy toward involved, invested members.

You deal with the bottom third by setting minimum standards for your organization and then holding all members to those minimum standards. *In order to be a member of this organization, you must do the following five basic things.* Make a list. What are the five things—OK, you can choose four or six, it doesn't really matter—that are the minimum expectations for everyone? Work on this list at your next retreat. What's the lowest level of involvement you could tolerate from a member?

If you do these five things and don't cause any problems, we will leave you alone. The list needs to be almost embarrassing. As a top-third member, you'll look at this list and be annoyed. You won't understand why someone would be a member of a group if this is all they want to do.

Show up to 50-percent of meetings.

Pay your dues on time.

Participate in our one big annual event in some capacity.

Keep a GPA of 2.0 or better.

Recommend one new member per year.

Come up with a list that makes sense for your organization.

A member who only wants this minimal level of involvement has made a choice. If that's all he wants, then fine. Call it the Good Enough Member job description. If you don't want to be a leader and you just want to be "good enough" to remain on the roster, then here you go. Do these five things, and we will leave you alone.

To make this work, however, you have to be willing to expel or remove those members who fail to meet even this embarrassingly small list of minimum expectations. Evaluate at the end of each semester. If a member isn't meeting the minimum expectations, he needs to leave the organization, voluntarily or involuntarily. If he causes drama or disruption, breaks the rules, or brings dishonor to the organization, he's gone. That simple.

Make sure everyone understands it. If you can't be a good enough member, then you won't be a member. Have a committee—or in a larger organization, formalize it as a "standards board"—to hold bottom-third members accountable to these minimum expectations.

Then, if a bottom-third member meets those minimums and doesn't cause trouble, leave that member alone. Don't chide and guilt her. Don't talk badly about her. Don't deny her the opportunity to participate in events. Let her exist quietly in the bottom third, and focus your energies elsewhere.

You never know. Sometimes that bottom-third member who chooses a minimum level of involvement might see something that inspires her to come back, increase her involvement, and start contributing again. Or, that member might just drift away quietly, never to be heard from again. You'll never fully understand why, and that's OK.

Focus on those who really want something out of the experience: the top- and middle-third members. Make their experience incredible, and make sure your organization is constantly improving for men and women who join in future years.

6

REASSURING AND SUPPORTING YOUR TOP THIRD

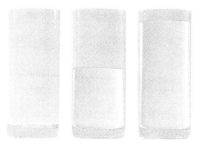

STUDENT organizations should be run for the benefit of those who enjoy them, believe in them, and work for them. As a student leader, you need to nurture your top-third and middle-third members, motivating them and rewarding them in ways that are appropriate. They are not the same, and as a savvy student leader, you need to understand that.

It's a much better idea to make the organization work for those who are committed to its success. Focus on those who choose to take part in a positive way, and stop worrying about convincing the bottom third to care as deeply as you do.

Allow some flexibility for middle-third members. Expect only the minimum from bottom-third members who wish to remain involved. Do these things, and you will see investment in your organization increase. You'll see your time and energy spent on more productive endeavors.

But, there's still one small problem.

Your top-third members might get very annoyed by the disparity in expectations. They will say it's not fair. They might wonder why members who put in very little get to attend the social events or ride on the Homecoming float or get access to the same benefits as they. You will try to elevate their rewards. You will give them lots of appreciation and praise. But, they'll still be annoyed.

When this happens, it's time for your top-third members to come to terms with a basic truth that will haunt them for the rest of their lives. *The idea that every member of an organization will be equally committed and engaged is a fantasy, and they are wasting their time whining about it.*

Many men and women in your organization will someday go on to work in companies where they will see the same dynamic. They will quickly see those employees who take the success of the company very personally, putting in extra hours and going the extra mile. Right alongside these high-achieving, top-third types will be others who are doing adequate or substandard work and who are simply punching the clock to get a paycheck. Some of these underachievers will be upper management, taking home big paychecks that far outweigh their benefit to the company.

It's not fair.

Many of your members someday will join a community of faith. They will see those who are passionately committed to studying their faith, assisting others and donating time and money to build up their congregation. Right alongside those folks will be those who simply go to services for show—who give almost nothing back and who incorporate very little of their faith's teaching in their lives.

These part-time believers will enjoy all the same social benefits of being a member, and it won't be fair.

Every person working in an office, every member of a church, every brother or sister of a fraternity/sorority, every honor society inductee, every player on a team—makes a choice. *How much am I going to commit to this?* Some will commit a lot, some will partially commit, and some will commit only the minimum necessary to enjoy the benefits.

It's not fair!

So then do you go through your life never committing to anything with a disproportionate level of commitment among members? If that's your strategy, you will live a very limited life where each night you go to bed frustrated.

It's an unavoidable reality. Some people give a damn. Some don't. And they all find themselves sharing space. As a committed member of an organization—as a self-selected student leader—you make a choice to give more. You choose to be a top-third member, because that's the choice that brings you the greatest happiness and sense of purpose.

In a healthy organization, the hardest working members also get extra benefits like self-satisfaction, deeper relationships and experiences, and a sense of contribution that far outweigh what the less committed members experience.

Work hard to make your top third feel valued. Make sure they get appreciation, benefits, and encouragement that match their level of output. But, also, be certain they understand the natural dynamics of an organization.

It's not going to be fair, ever, and we have to get beyond that. We have to be committed to excellence even when others around us inexplicably are not. Inspire them to give their best and to create the student leadership experience that fulfills them. If your organization can deliver that, your strongest members will stop complaining and will work even harder. They might even pity those who give less.

7

DISCUSSION

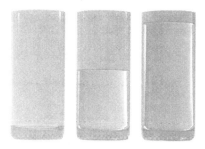

1. Take a list of your current members and divide it into thirds. Who are the top-third members who always show up and do a ton of work? Who are the bottom third who either cause problems or have a very weak commitment to the group? Who falls in the middle? (It's OK if it's not perfect thirds.)

2. Take a look at each name you've marked as a middle-third member. What are some positive ways this member contributes? What other priorities does this person have? What are some creative ways you can reduce the stress your middle member feels when the priorities conflict?

3. Middle members tend to love certain parts of your organization and like others less. For each middle member on your list, what does he/she love, and what does he/she enjoy the least? How can you give them more of what they love and less of what they dislike?

4. What is a major chronic issue that faces your group? How could you approach that issue in a new way using a Middle-Member Strategy?

5. What are some lower-pressure, supporting roles your organization could create that would appeal to middle members with more limited time to devote?

6. What can the officers and other top-third members do to bring middle members into decision-making processes more effectively?

7. How can you minimize the tension between the top third and the bottom third? This tension stresses out middle members the most.

8. What are the five to seven minimum standards you could put in place (Good-Enough Member job description) and enforce for those bottom-third members who want to retain their membership but do as little as possible?

9. When a new member joins your group, how can you best determine (or best guess) whether they will become a top-, middle- or bottom-third member?

10. Is there a certain group whose commitment level predictably drops? Seniors? Former officers? Why is this happening? How can your organization remain relevant to these members?

11. How do you make your top-third members feel appreciated for the work they do when they see middle- and bottom-third members contributing less? How can you convey the sense that the quality of their experience should not be determined by the commitment level of the bottom third?

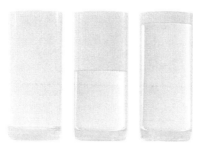

ACKNOWLEDGMENTS

Thank you to my team at CAMPUSPEAK, my brothers at Pi Kappa Phi Fraternity, and my colleagues in the world of fraternity and sorority advising who have supported my foolishness for more than two decades.

Durward Owen, my former boss, taught me the usefulness of viewing the world in thirds and many other lessons that have stuck with me.

Casey Cornelius, Lori Hart, Erin Weed and Cindy Kane gave feedback at critical moments and made this a better product. Special thanks to Q Digital Studios of Denver, photographer Keri Doolittle, and designer

Steve Whitby for keeping me visually interesting and current.

Personal thanks go to Mindy Sopher for the push to write, and above all to Dr. Scott Strong for the love, support and use of the dining room table.

ABOUT THE AUTHOR

T.J. Sullivan is the cofounder and CEO of CAMPU-SPEAK, the nation's premier agency providing educational speakers and workshops to college campuses. He is one of the best-known professional speakers on the college speaking circuit—speaking to more than two million students in all fifty states since 1992.

T.J. lives in Denver, Colorado.

Learn more at

www.tjsullivan.com

Follow T.J. on Twiter at

www.twitter.com/TJatCAMPUSPEAK

Find him on Facebook at

www.facebook.com/tjsullivanblog

Bulk purchases of this book for college courses or organizations may be made by contacting the author directly at sullivan@campuspeak.com or at 303-745-5545.

CPSIA information can be obtained at www.ICGtesting.com
Printed in the USA
BVOW050056281011

274548BV00001BA/74/P